AF885308

1st Civil No.
A137739 Division 4

IN THE COURT OF APPEAL OF THE STATE OF CALIFORNIA
First Appellate District
Division Four

SAMUEL H. SLOAN, Administrator of the Estate of K. Michael Goodall with Will Annexed

Objector and Appellant,

v.

SAM WARE,

Movant and Respondent,

and

Bank of America, N. A. Plaintiff

Appeal from an Order Removing Sam Ware as Counsel for the Estate of K. Michael Goodall,
San Francisco Superior Court,
The Honorable Peter J. Busch, Judge
Case No. PTR 99-273030

APPELLANT'S OPENING BRIEF

Samuel H. Sloan, en pro per
Administrator of Estate
of K. Michael Goodall
with Will Annexed
461 Peachstone Terrace
San Rafael CA 94903
(415) 419-5980
917-659-3397
samhsloan@gmail.com

PRELIMINARY STATEMENT

This is an appeal of an order withdrawing Sam Ware counsel for the Estate of K. Michael Goodall from appearing in this case. Counsel for the Goodall Estate sought to withdraw after counsel for Bank of America filed three successive motions for monetary sanctions. These motions were filed by Bank of America against Counsel for the Goodall Estate and personally against the administrator of the Goodall Estate with Will annexed. These successive motions for sanctions demanded that Counsel for the Goodall Estate and the Administrator of the Goodall Estate personally both pay between $13,000 and $16,000 to Counsel for Bank of America.

These three motions for sanctions were utterly frivolous and without basis. Their obvious propose was to frighten and intimidate counsel for the Goodall Estate and to scare him into not zealously presenting the best arguments and to frighten him so that he would not properly present the case and would not appeal if necessary. In view of this plus the obvious hostility of the judge presiding over the case to the rightful claims of the Goodall Estate, which made it likely that these motions for sanctions which threatened the professional career of Counsel for the Goodall Estate would be granted, he filed the motion to withdraw so as to get himself off the hook on these motions for sanctions. Even after filing the motion to withdraw, the comments by Judge Busch at the final hearing on sanctions show that Judge Busch was on the verge of ordering sanctions anyway. (See Record, Volume V, page 1685)

As much as we sympathize with the plight faced by Counsel for the Goodall Estate in a case where he had nothing to gain and everything to lose in the face of an obviously hostile judge, his withdrawal from the case left the Goodall Estate and the legitimate Goodall Heirs in an untenable position because the objective of Bank of America is to take the entire Goodall Estate and give it all to a charity they favor, namely Guide Dogs for the Blind. This would leave the legitimate Goodall heirs with nothing, zero.

Indeed, since then, Bank of America has filed three more cases in Marin County Superior Court against the Goodall Estate. The most recent case was filed just one month ago on March 19, 2013. These are Bank of America vs. Sloan, CIV 1203665, Bank of America vs. Sloan, CIV 1204541 and Bank of America vs. Sloan, CIV 1301196. All three of these cases are for the same purpose, to take possession of the Goodall Mansion. However, the first two cases were dismissed after the Marin County Superior Court ruled in favor of the Goodall Estate.

All of these cases plus the San Francisco case on appeal here are for the same purpose which is a collateral attack on the March 21, 2011 ruling and order of the Judge of the Marin County Probate Court who authorized the Administrator of the Goodall Estate, Samuel H. Sloan, to sell the Goodall Property, including the Goodall Mansion. (See Record, Volume I, page 293-294) Rather than directly contest and dispute the right of the Administrator of the Goodall Estate to sell the Goodall Mansion, Bank of America keeps filing cases in the wrong courts. At the last hearing in Marin County Superior Court on November 28, 2012, Judge Roy Chernus told Bank of America what they must do to take possession of the house, which is to file a claim to quiet title and this claim must be filed in Marin County, not in San Francisco. This is the very thing that Bank of America refuses to do.

As a result, because the San Francisco Superior Court judge withdrew Counsel for the Goodall Estate, Sam Ware, from this case, Sloan and the Goodall Heirs have approached dozens of other attorneys asking for legal representation. While there may be a phone book full of lawyers, none of the other attorneys will take this case for the obvious reason that the same thing that happened to Sam Ware will happen to them too. Nobody is willing to stick their head into the lion's mouth. Every attorney is afraid of what Bank of America will do to them if they take this case.

This means that the legitimate Goodall heirs cannot get proper legal representation. Appellant Samuel H. Sloan is not a lawyer. He is also not heir to the Goodall Estate. He took this case as a volunteer administrator because Mike Goodall was a lifelong personal special friend. They had been friends for fifty years since 1962 when they met at a chess tournament at Hamilton Air Force Base. Sloan agreed to become administrator of this estate at the request of the Goodall Heirs because none of them had the willingness or the capability to handle this complex case.

The motion filed by Sam Ware to withdraw as counsel gave only one reason for wanting to withdraw, which was "Concerns (describe the subject matter of the hearing) sanctions motion, cross motion". (See Record, Volume IV, page 1929). At the hearing on the motion, Sam Ware said the same thing. Here is what he said:

> Mr. Sloan and I just have a basic disagreement and have had a disagreement as to this motion for sanctions. I, quite frankly, I want to get out of it. When I got the papers from Bank of America that threatened sanctions, I thought, you know, I think it was

probably a good opportunity to avoid the sanctions issue, and I recommended that we, Mr. Sloan, withdraw the motion, and we had disagreement on that. And so not wanting to abandon Mr. Sloan, we went forward on that. But, you know, Mr. Sloan has kindly agreed that I can talk about that and appreciate that.

But he was very insistent that this thing go forward, this motion for reconsideration. But, you know, I think that's defensible within the realm of reasonable minds can differ as to the liability for that motion for reconsideration, and I will file a further opposition describing that. But the fact of the matter is that we disagree, disagreed

(See Record, Volume V, page 1663)

The reason counsel for the estate gave for wanting to withdraw, which was to get out from under the three motions for sanctions Bank of America had filed against him, is not a legally recognized reason for being allowed to withdraw. In addition, by doing so, counsel for the Goodall Estate has not merely abandoned Mr. Sloan. He has abandoned all of the Goodall heirs which include the two sisters and three brothers of Rachel

Goodall and their children and grandchildren, the two brothers of Kenneth Goodall, the two additional heirs of Michael Goodall and the putative child of Michael Goodall, for a total of 23 persons in all. All of these people will inherit nothing from the Goodall Estate if this order is not reversed. Accordingly, Appellant requests that this court reinstate Sam Ware as Counsel for the Estate.

In addition, Appellant requests this court to take plenary jurisdiction over this case. As will be shown, the San Francisco Superior Court lacked Jurisdiction over this case because the matter was already pending in Marin County Probate Court which had conducted hearings in this matter. All of the Goodall Property and all assets were in Marin County. The Goodalls all lived, died and are buried in Marin County. Their wills are all lodged in the clerk's office in Marin County Superior Court. In short, this case has nothing to do with San Francisco. It was filed here because for reasons best known to themselves Bank of America did not want to file this case in Marin County Probate Court and so they filed it in San Francisco Superior Court instead.

Secondly, Bank of America lacks standing to appear in this case. The Goodall Trust provides in Section 6.5(b) thereof, "The Trust Shall Terminate Upon Michael's Death". Michael died on

October 5, 2010, which is nearly three years ago. Under no circumstances is Bank of America the beneficiary of the estate. They have no claim at all. They want to award the assets of the Goodall Estate to Guide Dogs for the Blind. There is nothing in the trust documents that gives them the right to do that. If Guide Dogs for the Blind wants to claim to be the beneficiary of the estate, they should do that by filing their own petition. While the Guide Dogs have appeared in this case, they have never yet stated that they are entitled to inherit from the Goodall Estate, much less have they set forth the basis for their claims, if any. The petitions by Bank of America should be dismissed for lack of standing.

The assets of the Goodall Estate consist of an estimated $2 million dollars in cash and securities plus the Goodall Mansion at 461 Peachstone Terrace with an estimated value of $700,000. The cash amount is estimated because Bank of America refuses to provide any accounting of the funds, even though the trust documents clearly state that the accounting must be made to the heirs of the estate. (See the Record, Volume I, page 125) This includes all the Goodall Siblings. Rachel Goodall had two sisters and three brothers. Kenneth Goodall had two brothers. All of them are over 80. Most of them are still alive and have children and grandchildren actively involved and interested in this case. Bank of America has been completely stonewalling, refusing to provide any information to any of them.

Why does Bank of America fight like a dog over such a relatively small estate? The answer is perhaps that they have spent the money already. Certified financial statements show that at the time of the death of Col. Kenneth Goodall in 1994, the Goodalls had just slightly less than one million dollars in cash and securities. The trust dated September 12, 1990 did not put any of this money into the Trust. None of it was with Bank of America either. It was after Rachel Goodall died in June 1999 that Bank of America started contacting various financial institutions especially USAA Investment Management in San Antonio Texas demanding that these funds be transferred to Bank of America. These claims by Bank of America for the funds were without basis. Nevertheless, USAA Investment Management finally and with some reluctance transferred the funds to Bank of America. Thus, Bank of America essentially stole the money, because they had no right to it.

Having done that, Bank of America started charging monthly administration fees. The person receiving these administration fees was James R. Hastings who was attorney for Bank of America, the Goodalls and the Goodall Trust all simultaneously in an obvious conflict of interest. Then, when Mike Goodall sued Bank of America in December 1999 for doing this, the attorneys for Bank of America threatened him stating that if he kept fighting this case soon all the money would be exhausted in court and administration fees and Mike Goodall would be left with nothing.

Gary Rothstein, now Attorney for Bank of America, made the same threat to Sam Sloan, Administrator of the Estate. Rothstein stated that he charges $530 per hour in attorney's fees and if the Administrator, Sam Sloan, does not stop fighting this case the money will all soon be gone, as in Jarndyce v Jarndyce in Bleak House. However, this threat was ineffective here because it is evident that if the Goodall Estate does not win this case the money will all be exhausted any way. Indeed, Gary Rothstein recently told one of the Goodall heirs that the money is already completely spent and gone. There is no money left.

However, if Bank of America loses this case they will have to pay all this money back going back to the one million dollars they took from USAA Investment Management in 1999, plus interest from that day to this which will come to about two million. That is the reason Bank of America is fighting their meritless case so hard. This also lines the pockets of the attorneys representing Bank of America at their $530 hourly rate.

Appellant requests that this court reverse the decision of the court below thereby reinstating Sam Ware as Counsel for the

Estate and furthermore that this court dismiss this case as brought by Bank of America altogether for lack of standing and lack of jurisdiction and venue. If Bank of America has any claims to make, they should be directed to file those claims in Marin County Probate Court where the Goodall Estate Probate Case has been pending since February 1, 2011, long before Bank of America filed their petition in the instant case.

INTRODUCTION

This is an appeal from an order withdrawing the attorney for the Administrator of the Estate of K. Michael Goodall from this case.

This order was entered after extensive litigation that started in 1999 as indicated by the case number PTR 99-273030. The case under this number was originally filed by K. Michael Goodall represented by attorney Robert J. Rothman contesting the claims by Bank of America to be the Trustee of the Goodall Trust. The case never went to final judgment or conclusion because Mike Goodall simply ran out of money to pay Rothman's legal fees. Mike Goodall paid $7,000 to his attorney but that was soon exhausted. Nevertheless, Robert J. Rothman is still listed as counsel of record in this case to this day. Bank of

America has never served him with their pleadings, so he has not been drawn back into this case.

Meanwhile, Bank of America had invaded the account the Goodalls maintained with USAA Investment Management in San Antonio Texas which had about a million dollars in the account in 1999. The Bank of America somehow convinced USAA Investment Management to turn over the million dollars to Bank of America in January 2000, even while this case was pending. This constituted Grand Theft as Bank America had no legal right nor claim to the money. However, possession being 9/10ths of the Law, now Bank of America had the million dollars to pay its attorneys and Mike Goodall the rightful person to control the account had nothing and could no longer pay his lawyer, so the case became dormant. However, no final judgment has ever been entered.

On October 5, 2010, Mike Goodall died in the Goodall Mansion located at 461 Peachstone Terrace in San Rafael, California 94903. Samuel H. Sloan was in Khanty-Mansiysk, Siberia, Russia on that day attending the World Chess Olympiad. When he returned to San Rafael California in January 2011, he found Mike Goodall's last will and testament in his papers. He took that will down to Marin County Courthouse and filed it on January 28, 2011. Sloan filed a petition in probate on February 1, 2011. This petition was granted and Sloan was appointed

Administrator of the Estate with Will Annexed on March 21, 2011. (See Record, Volume I, page 293-294)

However, in the meantime, on or about February 28, 2011, Hamilton Kipp, an Employee of Bank of America, broke into and burgled the Goodall Mansion and removed the entire contents. The next day, March 1, 2011, when Sloan came home he found the entire mansion emptied of its contents and the locks on the doors changed. He found that a small back window had been left unlocked (apparently to allow the burglars to regain access if they wanted to return) so he crawled in that window and thereby regained possession of the house. He changed the locks on the doors back again. (See Record, Volume I, page 288-290)

However, everything was missing including not only the furniture but all the Goodall files, family records and legal documents. Sloan called 911 to report the burglary. Sheriff's Deputy Anthony Savas responded to the call. He said that he had seen a "Spanish Guy" with a dumpster removing the contents of the house. However, he refused to issue a police report for reasons unknown.

Sloan next went to the Marin County Sheriff's Department to complain. He was interviewed by a sergeant in the Sheriff's Department who said that if there was reason to believe that

Bank of America was involved they would not start a police case or issue a police report.

Sloan had no idea what had happened to the Goodall stuff. He called Gary Rothstein, Counsel for Bank of America, but Rothstein refused to give him any information. However, Sloan had an old girlfriend named Shanti Onofre who lived in Alameda. She attended an estate auction near her home in Alameda and by chance she noticed Mike Goodall's stuff being prepared to be auctioned off. She recognized the stuff, as she had been several times a guest in Mike Goodall's home in San Rafael.

In this way, appellant found out what had happened to the Goodall stuff. He confronted Gary Rothstein of Bank of America but Bank of America refused to return the Goodall stuff, even though some of the stuff was clearly the property of Mike Goodall personally or the property of the other residents in the Goodall House, Frank Thornally and Roy Hoppe.

With Bank of America stonewalling and refusing to return the stuff, Sloan filed an 850 motion to recover estate property in Marin County Probate Court. Bank of America in a telephone conference call hearing objected to the motion but the Probate Commissioner set it down for a hearing anyway. Finally, on June 10, 2011 on the eve of the hearing on the 850 Motion, Michaan's

Auction House, that had been holding the Goodall stuff in Alameda, substantially returned it to the Goodall Mansion.

Now, having lost twice in Marin County Probate Court although they had never filed a notice of appearance there, Bank of America did not do the proper thing, which was file their claims in the Marin County Probate Court (although it will be seen that they really do not have a legally cognizable claim of any kind). Instead, on April 21, 2011 Bank of America filed in San Francisco Superior Court a pleading entitled "Petition for an Order Confirming Real Property as an Asset of the Trust".

It was apparent that this petition went much further than the stated title. It gave as the caption of the case, "In the Matter of the Trust for Michael created under the Goodall Trust dated September 12, 1990". (See Record, Volume I, page 186)

However, that was not the caption of the case filed under that number. The real title of the case was "In Re The Goodall Trust". (See Record, Volume I, page 9). In addition, the trust is not a "Trust for Michael". The actual trust dated September 12, 1990 makes Michael Goodall the successor trustee of the Goodall Trust and not Bank of America. The actual Trust dated September 12, 1990 is the Record: (See Volume I, pages 105-130 and Volume IV, pages 1160-1185).

This trust makes Mike Goodall the Trustee, not Bank of America. Bank of America is nowhere mentioned in this document. Section 7.2 Page 119 makes Kenneth Michael Goodall the Successor Trustee and states on page 119 and 1175:

> "Kenneth Michael Goodall shall become the trustee. If Kenneth Michael Goodall is not qualified for appointment as trustee, or if he later dies, resigns or is removed pursuant judicial procedure or for any reason fails or ceases to act as trustee SECURITY PACIFIC BANK shall serve as the corporate sole trustee."

This particular point was raised at a hearing before Judge Roy Chernus in Marin County Superior Court on November 28, 2012. The following colloquy took place:

MR. SLOAN: Your Honor, this motion -- thank you for your tentative ruling, which I hope you accept. This motion is certainly not amenable for summary judgment at all. Every single issue of fact is in dispute.

For one thing, the number one fact is the Bank of America, the trustee of the Goodall Trust, in the 1990 trust document -- and I've included the full trust document in my motion papers -- does not name the Bank of America successor trustee; it names Security Pacific Bank as the successor trustee.

Secondly, he doesn't mention that there was also a second amendment to the Goodall Trust dated January of 1990 -- of 1999, making Michael Goodall the successor trustee succeeding his father. So when his mother died, there were two trustees: Michael Goodall and his mother. They were the trustees of the Goodall Trust. And when Rachel Goodall died, then Michael Goodall, by right, became the sole trustee of the Goodall Trust. And because Bank of America insisted they were the trustee, he filed a case against them on December 21st -- 27th, 1999, against the Bank of America. And that case was still going in litigation for 10 years, until he died on October 5th, 2010. So all these issues that he's saying are undisputed issues are disputed issues. They have been disputed the whole time.

And, secondly, as far as his statement about the documents, he has not yet -- we want discovery. They have not produced a single document since this case began. We have not seen that trust that he just said gives Bank of America -- makes them the trustee. They haven't produced that document. We want that document. We've made motions for that document, and we've served subpoenas for that document. We want depositions, especially of Hamilton Kipp and James Hastings. They won't agree to any discovery. The motion that they made was granted on a reply affidavit which they produced a document saying that Michael Goodall received something in the mail, but we didn't have even discovery to find out if he'd even answered it or if he really received it. So every single thing that he's talking about, these are things that are open to discovery and to issues of fact. I hope that you adopt the tentative ruling.

And by the way, I want to explain to Mr. Thornally and Mr. Hoppe, I'm the administrator of the estate. I was appointed by the probate judge here in Marin County. I don't know why they filed the case on the Goodall Trust in San Francisco when the proper venue and jurisdiction of this case was the same court, the same probate case that appointed me. They should not have been allowed to sue me in a different court than I was appointed from. I was appointed by the Marin County Probate Court, and they should have brought this case in Marin County. Why they should -- they should never have been allowed to bring the case over in San Francisco when all the people died here, they are buried here, their wills are lodged here in the clerk's office in Room 113. You can look up the wills of the Goodall parents and their son. They never had anything to do with San Francisco. They never went there. They didn't even like to cross the Golden Gate Bridge. And because he feels that they couldn't -- we had three hearings in Probate Court. I would have prevailed in all three hearings. And that's why they went over to San Francisco three months later and got a case over there, because they realized that they couldn't win here.

So I'm hoping that you will adhere to the tentative ruling. I'm also hoping that you will order discovery that they have to produce the documents which they claim to be relying on.

THE COURT: I don't issue -- there's not a motion for -- to compel discovery, as I'm hearing. I'm just hearing the summary judgment motions.

Anything else, sir?

MR. HOPPE: Okay. I was the -- Mike's roommate for 13 years at that place. I was also his caretaker the last couple of years. I don't know if that's relevant to this case or not. I also know what

Mike wanted.

THE COURT: Okay. That's not what I'm doing right now.

MR. HOPPE: Okay.

THE COURT: Okay. Thank you.

MR. HAHM: I'll make a couple of brief points, your Honor. And then I didn't address the motion with respect to Mr. Hoppe and Mr. Thornally, and I'd like to address that very, very briefly.

First, Security Pacific Bank became Bank of America back in 1991. We were the successor. You'll probably take judicial notice of it, but that was a very big transaction.

Number two, there was no form shopping when we initiated recently the Petition for Instructions in San Francisco Superior Court. We chose that venue because after Rachel Goodall died in 1999, Michael Goodall initiated a proceeding about the Goodall Trust in San Francisco. There was already a case opened there and, therefore, we filed our petition there.

In addition, ever since Rachel Goodall had passed away in 1999, Bank of America was the trustee of the Goodall Trust and had been operating under the assumption and belief that the house was an asset of that trust. So, again, if something had happened there, someone had been hurt, it wouldn't have been Michael Goodall who was responsible; it would have been the Goodall Trust. And as the trustee, Bank of America would be responsible for overseeing that. Bank of America, for example, would be the party that would initiate a quiet title action. If there was some sort of cloud on title -- if there was a neighbor, for example, who alleged he had an easement over the backyard, well, it would be Bank of America, as the trustee of the Goodall Trust which has the title to the property, that would initiate that UD action. What happened in San Francisco in the probate proceedings wouldn't change what the title is; it just allowed us to proceed as if it were an asset of the Goodall Trust.

And everything Mr. Sloan has said about disputes concerning documents, discovery, amendments to the Trust, this has all been presented to San Francisco Superior Court twice -- multiple times, I should say, in the probate proceedings. There has been adjudications against him. They should be final, number one, because the time to appeal them has elapsed. And I'm happy to brief that. I can demonstrate to your Honor very clearly

(See Record, Volume V, Pages 1704-1709)

As you can see from the above colloquy, Bank of America claims the right to be the trustee because they bought out Security Pacific Bank. However, Robert J. Rothman, as attorney for Mike Goodall, brought this point up too, saying that Bank of America was then purchased by a bank in North Carolina who then changed its name to Bank of America, so therefore the Bank of America today is not at all the same bank as the bank that existed by that name in 1990. (See Record, Volume I, page 180)

Thus this issue was raised at an early stage and Bank of America still has not responded. They have not explained how the purchase of the assets of Security Pacific Bank by Bank of America followed by the purchase of the assets of Bank of America by Nations Bank that then changed its name to Bank of America gave the current Bank of America the "right" to be the Trustee of the Goodall Trust.

More importantly, according to the Trust dated September 12, 1990, the bank only becomes involved "If Kenneth Michael Goodall is not qualified for appointment as trustee, or if he later dies, resigns or is removed pursuant judicial procedure or for any reason fails or ceases to act as trustee". (See Record,

Volume I, page 119). None of these things happened so Michael Goodall and not Bank of America was the rightful trustee.

Regarding the proceedings in Superior Court, there was no fact hearing in the superior court and no findings of fact. It is not true that these issues were heard and decided by the San Francisco Court. There was no sworn testimony, no declarations, no verifications, no evidence presented (because counsel for Bank of America said that the evidence had been lost). (See Record, Volume II, page 587-590) Thus, there was none of the things that normally accompany a judicial determination of facts.

This case is running in parallel in two different courts and these two courts have reached the opposite decisions. They know about each other and refuse to change their rulings so review by an appellate court is necessary. This case is running in parallel between two different courts in Marin and San Francisco, with opposite results. In the San Francisco case, the case is Case No. PTR 99-273030. In Marin County, the Case number is PRO1100596.

There has never been any discovery in this case except for a deposition of James R. Hastings in which he refused to produce any documents and he testified that he could not remember anything about this case and had lost or misplaced all his files of this case and so he had nothing to produce. (See Record, Volume II, pages 701-717)

In almost every instance, the issues in the San Francisco Case are exactly the same as the issues in the Marin Probate Case, yet the results have been the opposite. For example, the Bank of America filed a Statute of Limitations Claim in the Marin case. Judge Verna Adams dismissed that claim in a reasoned and lengthy opinion on April 16, 2012. Undaunted, Bank of America filed exactly the same claim in San Francisco, which resulted in an order from which an appeal was taken here.

Similarly, The Bank of America took the ruling by the San Francisco Court here and tried to enforce it over in Marin in a motion for summary judgment. However, the Marin County Superior Court Judge denied the claim by Bank of America, saying that the San Francisco order was interlocutory and non-final and thus non-enforcable in Marin. The Marin County judge ruled that Bank of America must file a claim to quiet title in Marin since the property is in Marin. However, throughout the two years that this litigation has been going on, Bank of America has been unwilling to submit its claims to the jurisdiction of the Marin courts, for reasons best known to Bank of America. This has resulted in this stalemate which will take action by the appellate courts to resolve.

Because of these conflicting decisions by different judges in different courts, the situation is in stalemate. The Goodall Estate consists of an estimated two million dollars in cash and securities plus a house known as "The Goodall Mansion" located at 461 Peachstone Terrace, San Rafael California 94903. Bank of America has all the money, having stolen it back in 1999 which resulted in this case, PTR 99-273030, whereas the Estate of Goodall has possession and control of the house. Bank of America has been unsuccessful in its efforts to oust the Goodall Estate from the house. Thus, it appears the parties will be locked in stalemate for an extended period of time, possibly even for years or forever.

The prior order dated May 16, 2012 was NOT a judgment. It did not use the word "judgment". It did not finally decide the action. It left unopened and undecided almost every question about this case. Indeed, the Bank of America moved to enforce this order over in Marin County Superior Court and Judge Roy Chernus there said that the May 16 order was NOT a final judgment and was interlocutory.

As Judge Roy Chernus of Marin County Superior Court stated in a one of the related cases in Marin County, "this is not your usual garden variety type of action" because while this case has been pending in the San Francisco Probate Court the same case has been pending over in the Marin County Probate Court. Two courts have been handling the same case.

Plaintiff here, Bank of America, lost their initial motions over in Marin County and then opted for the greener pastures in San Francisco Probate Court. As this case has progressed, every time Bank of America lost a motion over in Marin County they filed the same motion in San Francisco where they won.

Regarding the statute of limitations claim that Bank of America made in an "Additional Reply" in which the Administrator of the Goodall Estate did not have a chance to respond, Bank of America had made exactly the same Statute of Limitations claim in Marin County and Judge Verna Adams had dismissed that claim in a reasoned and lengthy opinion on April 16, 2012. Undaunted, Bank of America made that identical claim on San Francisco Probate Court.

Appellant was prevented by the actions of opposing counsel and actions of the judge which made it impossible for him to file an appeal any sooner than he did. Indeed, Appellant waited in the court room for the San Francisco Judge to sign his final order in this case so he could go down to the filing room to file his notice of appeal the same day.

In view of the actions of the San Francisco Probate Judge in making this case "Appeal Proof" by among other things waiting a full two months before signing the order denying the petition for rehearing, the judge prevented an earlier appeal. The order was submitted to the judge for signing on July 27, 2012. The judge did not sign it until September 26, 2012.

More than that, actions by Bank of America and Guide Dogs for the Blind unethically to chase Petitioner's Counsel off the case have made it impossible for Petitioner to retain new counsel. They did this by repeatedly filing motions for sanctions against existing counsel. Their first motion for sanctions which demanded attorneys fees between $13,000 and $16,000 against both the Administrator of the Goodall Estate and his counsel was filed on June 29, 2012. That motion was denied by Judge Busch on July 19, 2012.

However, on the very next day, July 20, 2012, Bank of America filed a second motion for sanctions even though nothing had changed overnight since the first denial.

A Third Motion for Sanctions was filed by Bank of America on August 14, 2012.

All these motions for sanctions filed by a big and powerful Bank of America and their counsel one of the largest law firms in California had the effect of understandably frightening the counsel for the Goodall estate. As no man can serve two masters, Counsel for the Goodall estate felt that he had to withdraw as counsel for the estate in order to defend himself against these successive motion for sanctions which threatened his professional career.

Meanwhile, Sam Sloan, the Administrator of the Goodall Estate, the Petitioner here, found it impossible to retain another counsel because every other attorney is afraid of Bank of America and their attorneys too. Nobody wants to stick their head in the lion's mouth.

As a result, Petitioner had no choice but to wait until these motions for sanctions and motion to withdraw were decided before he could file a notice of appeal. Petitioner was literally waiting in the courtroom for the judge to sign these orders so he could run down to the clerk's office and file his notice of appeal the same day.

After considering this matter, this court should dismiss this case entirely. The proper Probate Proceeding involving the Goodall Estate is now pending over in Marin County Probate Court. Case No. PR 1100596. The Goodall wills are admitted into probate in Marin. Everything about this case happened over in Marin. The only reason Bank of America filed in San Francisco is they do not like the judge over in Marin.

In addition, Bank of America should not have been allowed to use the case number of this inactive case to file a new claim for a different cause of action. There was no activity in this case for 11 years from March 2000 until April 2011. (See Record, Volume I, pages 185-186) This case should have been dismissed for inactivity under California Code of Civil Procedure Section 583.410. Thus this case should be dismissed with all orders vacated and Bank of America should be directed to file their claims in the right court, which is Marin County Probate Court.

We believe that the May 16, 2012 order is not a final judgment. It does not contain the word "Judgment". It does not include findings of fact and conclusions of law. It does not award money or property to anybody. It does not finally decide the action. However, the orders of the San Francisco Court cannot be ignored because Bank of America claims that it is a judgment and they have moved to enforce it as a judgment.

In August and October, 2012 Bank of America filed two unlawful detainer actions in Marin County seeking to evict the Goodall heirs and Goodall Estate from the Goodall Mansion at 461 Peachstone Terrace, San Rafael, California. These actions were unsuccessful, for the same reason Appellant has stated from the beginning. Judge Roy Chernus wrote in his ruling of November 28, 2012:

> "As against Sam Sloan and Kayo Kimura plaintiff seeks judgment for possession based on orders of the

San Francisco Superior Court and the July 27, 2012, Sixty-day notice. Plaintiff has put its title to the property "at issue" in this unlawful detainer proceeding. The bulk of the allegations in the Complaint and the "Undisputed Facts" in support of the subject motion for summary judgment are addressed to plaintiffs extensive efforts by way of collateral proceedings in San Francisco Superior Court to confirm that the premises is an asset of the Trust for Michael created under the Goodall Trust dated September 12,1990, that title to the premises is in Bank America as trustee, and that plaintiff may administer the premises pursuant to the terms of Trust.

Yet despite plaintiffs extensive allegations detailing the San Francisco proceedings, plaintiff does not actually allege or demonstrate via undisputed facts that the orders of the SF Sup. Court are final or that the issue of its title to the subject property has been fully and finally determined.

Plaintiff appears to base its right to commence this unlawful detainer proceeding upon the Minute Order of the SF Superior Court dated July 19, 2012, denying defendant's petition for reconsideration as plaintiff served the subject 60-Day Notice eight days later on July 27,2012, even though the court's order was not formally entered until September 27, 2012. (See Complaint, par. 19, and Exh. E) Even assuming the order denying defendant's petition for reconsideration constitutes a final and binding determination of plaintiffs title (though not specifically alleged) plaintiff served the 60-day notice before that order was formally entered on September 27, 2012. This unlawful detainer action was filed a mere 12-days later on October 9, 2012. As stated by the Court in Greenhut v. Wooden {1982} 129 Cal.App.3d 64,68, this is not your usual garden variety type of unlawful detainer action where the issue of title is strictly limited. Having put its own title in issue and by relying on the San Francisco Trust proceeding as the source of its authority to commence this proceeding plaintiff should demonstrate that title to the property has, in fact, been finally adjudicated in its favor. Plaintiff's pleading and evidence falls short of demonstrating a final adjudication of title in its

> favor and raises a question of fact whether the alleged 60-day notice was served prematurely.
>
> As to defendants Hoppe and Thornally, a complaint for unlawful detainer must allege that the tenant continues in possession of the premises. (CCP $1161.) No cause of action for unlawful detainer exists if the tenant has quit before the action is filed. Defendants Hoppe and Thornally have filed answers admitting they have relinquished possession of the premises. In its motion, plaintiff claims that while Hoppe and Thornally have relinquished physical possession of the premises, "plaintiff is informed that Hoppe and Thornally have not relinquished their alleged right to possession of the premises." If a landlord wishes to determine rights to possession but not physical possession, it cannot do so by way of summary unlawful detainer; a quiet title action would be the proper remedy."

Thusly, Judge Chernus stated in essence the same thing petitioner Sloan has been saying from the first pleading which is that the only way for Bank of America to get what it wants is to file a petition in Marin County. Bank of America can never succeed in obtaining access to real property in Marin by bringing cases in San Francisco.

This action by Bank of America should be dismissed and thrown out of court for a deeper reason, which is that Bank of America has never had standing in this case. Bank of America was never the legal trustee of the Goodall Trust. Kenneth and Rachel Goodall were the trustees. Upon the death of Kenneth, the Trust documents show that Michael became the co-trustee with his mother and upon her death Michael became the sole trustee. The documents showing this are annexed as exhibits here. At no time did Bank of America have any rights in this case. They simply usurped and stole this case because of the millions of dollars involved. What happened is Bank of America stole the money, pure and simple. They have no right and no claim to the Goodall assets.

In addition, Guide Dogs for the Blind has no standing and no claim. The trust document upon which Bank of America and Guide Dogs for the Blind relies (although they have failed and refused to produce it and claimed to have lost it) does not establish their right.

Paragraph 6 of the petition filed by Bank of America contains the following noteworthy statement.

> No title documents have been found placing title in the residence in the name of petitioner [Bank of America] as Trustee of the Trust for Michael." (See Record, Volume I, page 189)

What Bank of America was asking here was that the title to the Goodall Mansion be changed by order of the San Francisco Superior Court. However, as Appellant Sloan pointed out in his pro se answer to this petition, "It is HORNBOOK Law that any proceeding involving real property must be filed in the jurisdiction where the property is located." (See Record, Volume I, page 287)

Paragraph 6, note 1 of the petition filed by Bank of America contains another noteworthy statement.

> "The Provisions of the Bypass Trust are somewhat unclear with respect to the proper beneficiaries of the Trust for Michael in the wake of Mike Goodall's Death." (See Record, Volume I, footnote at the bottom of page 189)

"Somewhat unclear" is a massive understatement or misstatement. The trust documents have been shown to several attorneys specializing in such matters. All them say that the trust documents are nonsense. "Absurd", "ridiculous" and several other adjectives are used to describe these trust documents. A well known San Francisco attorney said that the attorney who drew up this trust should be disbarred for incompetence.

Michael Goodall died on October 5, 2010 in his home known as "The Goodall Mansion" at 461 Peachstone Terrace in San Rafael, Marin County, California. Petitioner found the Goodall Will among his papers and filed it in Marin County Probate Court on January 28, 2011. On February 1, 2011, Petitioner filed a petition in probate. After consents were obtained from all of the heirs of the Goodall Estate, petitioner petitioned and after two hearings was appointed administrator of the estate.

Petitioner had the key to the house, as he has been a resident of the house. However, on February 28, 2011, while petitioner was away for a few days, there was a break-in and burglary in the house. The entire contents of the house was removed including all legal papers and documents of the Goodalls. When the burglary was discovered, 911 was called and this was reported as a burglary. Deputy Anthony Savas of the Marin County Sheriff's Department responded to the call. Deputy Savas said that he had been patrolling the area during the previous days and had observed a large trash dumpster in front of the house with a Spanish guy bringing stuff out of the house and putting it in the dumpster. However, Deputy Savas had not stopped to inquire, as this had seemed to be a routine case of somebody moving out.

On April 21, 2011, Bank of America by way of collateral attack had filed a petition in San Francisco Superior Court seeking essentially to overturn the Marin County Probate Order which had listed among other things the Goodall Mansion as an asset of the Goodall Estate. In filing this new petition, Bank of America had used an old case number, PTR 99-273030. That was the number of a case Michael Goodall had filed in December 21, 1999 shortly after his mother had died in which he sought the removal of Bank of America as Trustee on many grounds including the grounds that Bank of America was not the bank named in the Trust documents and that the proper trustee was Michael Goodall himself and if not himself then at least some bank not openly hostile to him as Bank of America was.

Page 18 of a trust document, which Bank of America claims has been lost but they claim is controlling, but which we are prepared to prove was never signed by any of the Goodalls, especially since Col. Goodall was hospitalized and on his death bed with Esophageal cancer, had a feeding tube inserted in his abdomen and was unable to speak, contains the following provision:

> "(d) If MICHAEL does not survive the surviving settler and leaves no issue who survive the surviving settler, the trustee shall distribute the trust property twenty thousand dollars ($20,000) to each of the then living brothers and sisters of the trustor RACHEL A. Goodall and the remainder to GUIDE DOGS FOR THE BLIND OF MARIN, INC., of San Rafael California."

The problem is that this provision only applies if Michael dies BEFORE his parents do. However, Mike survived his parents by 11 years. Kenneth F. Goodall was born 01 Mar 1916 and died 10 Sep 1994 at age 78. His Social Security Number was 444-40-8884. Rachel A. Goodall was born 23 May 1916 and died 07 Jun 1999. Her Social Security Number was 359-07-1738. Kenneth Michael Goodall was born 13 Jan 1946 and died 05 Oct 2010. His Social Security Number was 559-70-3352.

Since Mike Goodall died 11 years after his parents did, that paragraph does not apply. More than that, nowhere in the entire document, 40 pages long, is there any mention of what happens if Mike dies after his parents do, except that the trust documents state that the trust terminates upon the death of Mike Goodall.

This provision and the entire document makes it completely 100% clear that the Goodall Estate belongs entirely to Mike Goodall and his heirs, unless Mike Goodall dies before his parents do. There is no possible way that Guide Dogs for the Blind gets anything out of the Goodall Estate. Under no interpretation of the Goodall Trust does Guide Dogs for the Blind get anything.

Yet, Bank of America, in its initial petition filed in San Francisco Superior Court, said that it was due to drafting errors that the trust documents mistakenly do not give any money to Guide Dogs for the Blind. Bank of America asked the Superior Court to in effect rewrite the trust documents so as to have the Goodall Estate go to the Dogs.

At the first hearing in San Francisco Superior Court on May 25, 2011, Petitioner appeared *in pro per* because he felt it absurd and ridiculous that Bank of America would file their petition, because the trust documents clearly DO NOT give any part of the Goodall Estate to the Dogs and secondly because this case was already pending as a probate case in Marin County that clearly had jurisdiction. The Goodalls all lived and died in Marin County, all of their property including their house was in Marin County, all their documents were executed in Marin County and there was nothing about this case that had anything to do with San Francisco County. Thus, San Francisco County obviously does not have jurisdiction. Petitioner expected that the San Francisco Court would throw the case out immediately.

In addition, Guide Dogs for the Blind is behind all of the other heirs. The trust provides that each of the Goodall siblings gets $20,000. Rachel Goodall had five siblings, three brothers and two sisters, and Kenneth Goodall had two brothers. Many of them are dead but they all married and had children, some of whom were adopted. There are twenty-three Goodall heirs listed on the service list and they all have the right to contest this case. Clearly, only the Marin County Probate Court has the jurisdiction, venue and competence to decide these claims.

In addition, the direct heirs of Michael Goodall have a claim. The trust provides that his wife and/or children inherit from the trust.

Guide Dogs for the Blind are at the bottom of the totem pole. This case goes to the Dogs and they get money only after all of these other people and even then the Dogs do not get anything unless Michael dies before either of his parents do, which did not happen.

Because of all these factors, Appellant assumed that the San Francisco case would either be dismissed or else transferred to the right court, which was Marin County Probate Court. Petitioner was thus shocked when the San Francisco judge with a wave of the hand and without giving any reason for the decision or indeed without saying anything at all ruled in favor of Bank of America and signed an order that had been handed up without even allowing the Petitioner to see and comment on the order that was being signed.

Appellant then realized that he had better retain counsel. After a long search, Appellant found a qualified attorney, Sam Ware, willing to represent the Goodall Estate on a Contingency Fee basis. This was necessary because Bank of America had already taken all the money. Col. Kenneth and Rachel Goodall had never had an account with Bank of America, not even a simple checking account. Col. Goodall was retired military officer, so most of the Goodall money was with USAA Investment Management in San Antonio, Texas. They also had smaller amounts with mutual funds and stock trading accounts. None of this was with Bank of America or anywhere in the state of California.

Right after Rachel Goodall had died in June 1999, Bank of America through its attorney James R. Hastings had contacted USAA Investment Management and directed that all Goodall funds be transferred to Bank of America. Mike Goodall had not been told about this and had no idea that this had happened. In short order, all of the bank accounts that Mike Goodall had been operating under power of attorney were stripped of their assets. Mike Goodall was left destitute and without funds. That is the reason why he filed this case on December 21, 1999.

Bank of America completely stonewalled, as they continue to do this day. They refused and still continue to refuse to give Mike Goodall or indeed any of the Goodalls any accounting or any information about what happened to the Goodall Millions. It was as if the funds had disappeared into a Black Hole.

Just before Col. Kenneth Goodall died in 1994, he had an accounting done of the funds. The accounting shows that the Goodalls had slightly less than one million dollars in cash and securities plus the fully paid for house. Rachel Goodall was an excessively frugal person. She basically never spent money on anything, so the money should at least have doubled since 1994.

After the adverse ruling on May 25, 2011, Petitioner was able to retain counsel in time for the next hearing in San Francisco Probate Court. Meanwhile, several hearings on the same subject matter had been held in Marin County Probate Court.

It is important at all times to remember that this case is running in parallel in two different courts: San Francisco Superior Court and Marin County Probate Court. Obviously, the

Marin County Court is the right court and at each hearing in San Francisco Petitioner has demanded transfer of this case to Marin.

At the next hearing in San Francisco, Bank of America brought attorney James R. Hastings to court prepared to have him testify as a witness, as he had been attorney for both the Goodalls, the Goodall Trust and the Bank of America. Hastings was going to testify that the money should go to the Dogs. This was one of just many obvious conflicts on interest by James R. Hastings. However, Petitioner's new counsel Sam Ware asked for the opportunity of discovery. Bank of America protested vehemently and said that there should be no discovery at all. They especially objected to any discovery of the money. They refused to reveal anything about the Goodall millions, how much it was, were they had gotten it from and what they had done with it.

Finally, Judge Mary Wiss agreed that there should be some discovery. Whereas Bank of America wanted to hold a hearing and finish the case that day, the superior court judge said that there should be discovery.

However, as will be seen, there has never been any discovery on this case, because Bank of America has been completely stonewalling. Not one document has been produced either by Bank of America or by attorney James R. Hastings. Bank of America has absolutely refused to produce anything. James R. Hastings has testified that he has lost the files and thus does not have anything. In addition, he has stated that to provide any discovery would violate the attorney Client Privilege of Bank of America because he was counsel for Bank of America at the same time that he was counsel for the Goodalls. (See Record, Volume II, page 570)

Sam Ware then subpoenaed James R. Hastings for a deposition and required him to bring all documents and files pertaining to this case. Hastings appeared for the deposition on November 14, 2011 but did not bring any documents at all. His attorney Don Lesser said that the subpoena was overbroad and as Hastings had been attorney for Bank of America too it would violate the attorney client privilege of Bank of America and that the files and notes pertaining to this case had all been lost. At the oral deposition, Hastings testified that basically he could not remember anything about the case. (See Record, Volume II, page 542-558)

On December 14, 2011, Sam Ware filed a motion for discovery and production of documents pertaining to this case. On December 29, 2011, Don A. Lesser, Counsel for James Hastings, filed opposition to the motions for discovery, saying that it would be "oppressive and burdensome" upon James R. Hastings and also violate the attorney client privilege of Bank of America because James R. Hastings had been attorney for Bank of America at the same time that he was attorney for the Goodalls and the Goodall Trust. (See Record, Volume II, page 570)

Not long thereafter Don Lesser withdrew as counsel for James R. Hastings, but without filing a notice of withdrawal with the Superior Court, even though he had appeared in the case.

On January 20, 2012, Judge Busch denied the motion for production of documents, especially the trust document, but said that James R. Hastings was required to search his files to look for the trust and if he could find it he was required to produce it and otherwise he must file a declaration stating what efforts he had made to find the trust.

On February 2, 2012, James R. Hastings filed a declaration stating that he had searched all his files and was unable to find the trust. (See Record, Volume II, page 612-613)

On February 6, 2012, Nancy Rodgers, a friend and neighbor of the Goodalls, filed a declaration stating that her purported witness signatures on the Goodall Wills, which were pour over wills pouring money into the trust, were not her signatures and she had never signed any such documents. As there had never been any money in the trust, these pour over wills were essential to the claims by Bank of America and Guide Dogs for the Blind to be entitled to any of the Goodall millions. (See Record, Volume II, page 652-653)

After several more pleadings were filed on all sides, on April 24, 2012, Bank of America filed an additional reply asserting for the first time in this case that objections to the 1994 Trust were time-barred by a Statute of Limitations. (See Record, Volume III, page 925) Although this was the first time Bank of America had made this claim in this case, they had made exactly the same claim in the parallel proceeding going on in Marin County Probate Court. That claim had been dismissed by Marin County Probate Judge Verna Adams in a lengthy and reasoned decision on April 16, 2012. The statute of limitations claim was also entirely bogus and ridiculous for several reasons the most obvious being that Michael Goodall had indeed contested the right of Bank of America to be the trustee by filing this very case on December 21, 1999. Also, the statute of limitations claim was not accompanied by any evidence or a declaration in support. In addition, the words "as amended" had been omitted or when it was included, obviously it logically referred to the 1999 Amendment to the Trust which had made Mike Goodall the Trustee. The 1990 Trust had made Michael Goodall the beneficiary of the trust and the 1999 Amendment had made Michael the co-trustee of the trust, so there was no reason for Michael to object to either of them. (See Second Amendment to the Goodall Trust in the Record, Volume II, pages 55-57)

Because of the shortness of time before the previously scheduled hearing, Samuel Sloan and his counsel did not have time to respond to this "additional reply" and so asked for additional time which was denied from the bench. And so, Judge Busch signed the order dated May 16, 2012 from which the first appeal is taken, without a fact hearing of any kind and without any findings of fact or conclusions of law. (See Record, Volume III, page 937)

On May 25, 2012, seven days after the entry of the order of May 16, 2012, Samuel Sloan filed through counsel a motion for discovery to compel the production of documents including the documents forming the basis of the newly made statute of limitations claim. This was not filed as a motion for reconsideration, because Sloan through counsel deemed the May 16, 2012 order to be an interlocutory order, not a final judgment, because, among many other things it does not use the word "judgment", and does not dispose of all of the issues involved in this case. However, this motion was filed within the time limit for motions for reconsideration to be on the safe side in case the courts were later to decide that it was a judgment. (See Record Volume III page 970)

Sam Sloan, Administrator of the Goodall Estate, had been caught off guard by the May 16, 2012 decision because he had naturally assumed that there would be some sort of trial or fact hearing and Bank of America would be required to present their evidence if any before the court would rule. It was not to be expected that the judge would decide this complicated case abruptly from the bench without any hearing. Because of this surprise ruling, the administrator started searching through the 40 or 50 storage boxes of material Bank of America had stolen when they broke into the Goodall Mansion on February 28, 2011 but then were forced to return on June 10, 2011 by proceedings in the Marin County Probate Court.

During these searches, the administrator found a treasure trove of documents. All or almost all of these documents had been prepared by James R. Hastings, Attorney for Bank of America, so Bank of America had these documents all along but had failed to produce them. Of great importance was a Power of Attorney the Goodall Parents, Kenneth and Rachel Goodall, had given their son Michael on August 24, 1994 on the Death Bed of Kenneth, placing Michael with power of attorney over the Goodall Trust. (See Record, Volume III, pages 977-993) This proved that the claim by the Attorney of Bank of America that the Goodall parents did not trust Michael with their money was false. Also included in the same treasure trove of documents was a signed health care directive by Kenneth Goodall that he be allowed to die of the Esophageal cancer of which he was suffering at the time (See Record, Volume III, pages 955-966) and an unsigned 1994 Goodall Trust showing that Kenneth had never signed the 1994 amendment to the trust. Kenneth Goodall was in the final stages of cancer and a feeding tube had been inserted in his abdomen on July 17, 1994. He died on September 10, 1994. These documents were included in the exhibits Sloan filed in his May 25, 2012 motion.

On the same date, Sloan filed a declaration of David S. Moore, a highly regarded forensic document examiner, who stated that upon comparing the known and authentic signatures of Kenneth Goodall found on other documents, on checks, on his personal notebook and the like and comparing them with the signature on the purported 1994 amendment to the trust, they were not consistent but he could not made a final determination as to whether the signature was authentic or not without being allowed to examine the actual trust document, but such an examination had been denied. (See Record, Volume III, pages 955-966)

Included among the documents given to David S. Moore for examination is an extensive handwritten notebook maintained by

Col. Kenneth F. Goodall showing his plans and intentions regarding his death and the Goodall Trust. This notebook shows that it was his intention that only the house would be in the trust, not the money. It was also his intention that if Michael Goodall married or had children, they would inherit from the trust. The Goodall parents were actively encouraging their son to get married and start raising a family. They were certainly not going to create a trust that would disinherit their son and his future wife and children. Administrator Sam Sloan brought this notebook with him to court every time this case was set for a hearing. However, Judge Busch by denying any hearing on this matter prevented the Goodall Estate from offering this notebook and the conclusive proof that it contains into evidence. The notebook is still today in the possession of David S. Moore, forensic document examiner.

On June 27, 2012, Gary Rothstein, attorney for Bank of America, served on Sam Sloan and his counsel Sam Ware a motion for sanctions against the Motion for Discovery dated May 25, 2012 asking for sanctions against Sam Sloan personally and against Sam Ware personally in the amount of $13,596 for filing the motion for discovery which they deemed to be a motion for reconsideration. In a cover letter, Gary Rothstein, attorney for Bank of America, stated that unless the motion for reconsideration were withdrawn he would file the motion for sanctions, effectively blackmailing the Goodall Estate.

It is important to remember here that Sloan is a volunteer administrator of the trust because the Goodall Trust has no money because Bank of America stole it all and Sloan is not named in the will. In addition, Attorney Sam Ware took this case as a contingency case. By serving this motion for sanctions, Bank of America was threatening Sloan and his counsel with a substantial financial loss of $13,596 whereas they had nothing to gain from this case. (Record, Volume III, page 1088)

So, the Administrator of the Goodall estate had everything to lose and nothing to gain by continuing this case.

Nevertheless, the administrator and his counsel did not Cave in yet.

On June 29, 2012 Guide Dogs for the Blind joined this motion by filing their own motion for sanctions for filing this petition for rehearing. (See Record Volume III page 1060)

A hearing was held on these motions on July 19, 2012. Judge Busch denied the motion which he deemed to be a motion for reconsideration and he also denied the motion by Bank of America and Guide Dogs for the Blind for Sanctions against the Administrator of the Goodall Estate and Sam Ware, Counsel for the Goodall Estate.

On July 20, 2012, the very next day, Bank of America filed a new motion for Sanctions against the Administrator of the Goodall Estate and against Sam Ware Counsel for the Goodall Estate seeking sanctions in the amount of between $13,000 and $16,000 against each of them. This motion had been denied from the bench the previous day so obviously nothing had changed. (See Record, Volume III, pages 1079-1088)

On July 27, 2012, the parties submitted for the judge's signature an order denying the motion for reconsideration heard on July 19, 2012. Sam Sloan, Administrator of the Estate, planned and intended to file a notice of appeal as soon as the order was signed. Instead the judge sat on the order for two full months and did not sign it until September 26, 2012. It was entered the following day. This delay of two months put it past the normal time for filing a notice of appeal. (See Record, Volume IV, pages 1308-1312)

On August 14, 2012, Bank of America filed a third Motion for Sanctions against the Administrator of the Goodall Estate and his attorney. (See Record, Volume III, pages 1110)

On September 7, 2012, as a result of having three successive motions for sanctions filed against him, Sam Ware filed a motion to be relieved as counsel. He said that he could not effectively oppose the repeated motions for sanctions against him while also acting as counsel for the estate. No man can serve two masters so he needed to be relieved as counsel so that he could defend himself against actions by Bank of America and their counsel which threatened his professional career.

Now again Sloan could not file his notice of appeal because he had to wait until the judge decided the motion for sanctions and the motion by his counsel to withdraw to escape the sanctions. As Sloan was represented by Counsel, he could not file the Notice of Appeal by himself. In addition, as these motions affected the merits of the case and the judge was retaining jurisdiction over the case, there remained the possibility that the judge would reverse himself and the case would continue.

Finally, the judge held his hearing on the motion to withdraw which was strenuously opposed by Sloan and granted the motion on November 15, 2012. On the same day, Judge Busch held his hearing on the motion for sanctions and denied that motion, basically saying that there was enough grounds for Counsel for the Goodall Estate to file a motion for reconsideration but not enough grounds for him to grant it.

On November 21, 2012, Judge Busch signed the order denying the Motion for Sanctions. Sloan filed his notice of appeal the very same day.

ARGUMENT

The immediate issue before the court is the motion to withdraw as counsel. Appellant has attempted to research the case law on this and has found no case in which an attorney was allowed to withdraw under the circumstances here. The sole reason given in the motion to withdraw was concern about the motion for sanctions. However, the threat of sanctions is not grounds to withdraw from a case. Otherwise, in every case an aggressive litigant could easily chase opposing counsel off a case.

A reason he gave at the hearing was "disagreements" about whether to file the petition for rehearing. He obviously said this to get himself off the motion for sanctions. One can see by a perusal of the record that includes many documents written, signed and filed by Sam Ware, that he substantially agreed with the views of the Administrator Sam Sloan about this case. On one point, he was not willing to go as far. Although the Administrator of the Estate, Sam Sloan, declared the signature on the purported trust dated August 24, 1994 (just 17 days before Col. Kenneth Goodall died) to be "a forgery", this was based on the fact that he knew the Goodall Family for 50 years plus he had access to their personal notes, letters and files. He also knew Mike Goodall well enough to know that he would have never gone against the wishes of his parents. The attorney Sam Ware never met the Goodalls, and so could not be as sure about this, but he did question the authenticity of the document and demanded that it be produced. The Bank of America refused to produce the document and said that it had been lost. So, the result was the same regardless of whether it was "a forgery" or merely "not authentic".

Attorneys often have disagreements with their clients. A mere disagreement is not grounds to withdraw. Attorney Sam Ware did not do anything different from what Sam Sloan asked him to do. Sam Sloan expressed satisfaction with his representation and wanted him to continue and by this appeal is asking that he be reinstated.

In addition, the real client is the Goodall Estate, not Sam Sloan personally. Sam Ware has an obligation to represent the interests of all 23 Goodall heirs. Thus, if this court fails to reverse the decision of the court below, all 23 heirs will be left without legal representation. Counsel for Bank of America recently stated that the bank has spent all the Goodall money, the entire two million, and there is nothing left. So, the Goodall heirs will receive nothing unless this order is reversed.

Appellant has approached more than a dozen qualified attorneys asking them to represent the estate and all have declined. They all give much the some reason. They can see that any attorney who undertakes to represent the Goodall Estate will be attacked by Bank of America, much as Sam Ware has been attacked by Bank of America here.

Meanwhile, the case is far from over. We believe that the May 16, 2012 order is not a final judgment. It does not contain the word "Judgment". It does not include findings of fact and conclusions of law. It does not award money or property to anybody. Last month Bank of America filed a new case against the Estate in Marin County Superior Court and last week counsel for Bank of America said he is getting ready to file a new motion in the case presented here in San Francisco Superior Court.

Clearly, the Estate needs to get legal representation, not just an in pro per non-lawyer like Sam Sloan, but we cannot get representation if this order is not reversed.

Going further, this case should be dismissed altogether. The case under this number PTR 99-273030 was filed by Michael

Goodall on December 21, 1999 demanding the removal of Bank of America as Trustee of the Trust. The attorney for Michael Goodall was Robert J. Rothman.

The last document filed by Rothman was entitled "Points and Authorities in Support of Petition to Remove Trustee". (See Record, Volume I, page 179) It was filed on March 21, 2000. No response was ever filed by Bank of America. Unfortunately, at that point Mike Goodall ran out of money to pay his lawyer. We now know what would have happened had he paid more money. He would have paid and paid and paid until whatever money he had ran out, as Bank of America and its attorneys was prepared to fight like tigers to the end to keep this estate and to get the Goodall Millions.

Then 11 years passed during which nothing happened in this case. Then, on April 21, 2011, eleven years and one month later, Bank of America filed its "Petition for Order Confirming Real Property as an Asset of the Trust". (See Record, Volume I, page 186). They used the old case number to file a new case for the opposite cause of action. They did this specifically to avoid filing in Marin County Probate Court where the Goodall Estate had been admitted to probate months earlier. Their petition states on its face that the purpose is to change the title to the Goodall Residence and in effect to collaterally attack the order of the Marin County Probate Court dated March 21, 2011. (See Record, Volume I, page 187) In his decision on November 28, 2012, Judge Roy Chernus of Marin County Superior Court stated exactly that, that the San Francisco petition was filed for purpose of collateral attack.

Appellant had filed a motion for discovery. The superior court had ruled in favor of a new claim by Bank of America that a Statute of Limitations barred petitioner's defense. This claim was obviously bogus because Mike Goodall had filed this very case back in 1999 to object to Bank of America being the trustee.

The judge delayed two months in signing the order. This delay of two months by the judge was what put the case over the time limit to file the appeal. The order was submitted to the judge for signing on July 27, 2012. The judge did not sign it until September 26, 2012.

The order that Judge Busch signed had not been after proper notice and opportunity for a hearing. Indeed, there has never been a fact hearing in this case. There has never been sworn testimony of any witnesses. There has been no discovery. No documents have been produced by Bank of America. Hastings says that he has lost the trust documents. If you look at the case files you will see that there have been no declarations, no exhibits, no verifications, no findings of facts and no conclusions of law.

Neither Bank of America nor Guide Dogs for the Blind have ever filed a brief or a memorandum of law in this case. They have never cited a single case, they have never explained upon what legal grounds or theory of law they are entitled to proceed. They have not even explained what they are even doing appearing in this case as the last of the Goodalls died more than two years ago. They have no standing to be appearing in this case. Only the contestants, namely Guide Dogs and the legitimate heirs have standing.

Meanwhile, James R. Hastings, who says that he has lost the documents, is teaching a class in Estate Planning. On page 15 of the current Tamalpais Union High School District Summer Camp Sneak Preview there is an ad for the next course by James Hastings. It is called Estate Planning 101. The next class started on April 23, 2013 and the fee to attend the class is $25.

At a hearing in Marin County Superior Court on November 28, 2012 in which Bank of America sought to enforce the order from which an appeal was taken, Judge Roy Chernus ruled that the May 2012 order was not a final judgment and was interlocutory.

According to that ruling, appeal is unnecessary. However, Bank of America disagrees. They consider May 2012 the San Francisco order to be the final judgment. As a result this case is stalemated.

The actions of the San Francisco Superior Court Judge attempted to make this case "Appeal Proof" by among other things waiting a full two months before signing the order denying the petition for rehearing. The order was submitted to the judge for signing on July 27, 2012. The judge did not sign it until September 26, 2012.

More than that, actions by Bank of America and Guide Dogs for the Blind unethically made it impossible for Petitioner to retain new counsel. They did this by repeatedly filing motions for sanctions against existing counsel. Their first motion for sanctions which demanded attorneys fees between $13,000 and $16,000 against both the Administrator of the Goodall Estate and his counsel was filed on June 29, 2012. That motion was denied by Judge Busch on June 19, 2012.

After considering this matter, this court should dismiss this case entirely. The proper Probate Proceeding involving the Goodall Estate is now pending over in Marin County Probate Court. Case No. PR 1100596. Everything about this case happened over in Marin County. The only reason Bank of America filed in San Francisco is they do not like the judge over in Marin.

CONCLUSION

For all of the reasons Set forth above, the decision and order of the court below must be reversed and this case should be dismissed entirely.

This document is prepared in Courier New Bold 12 point with a word count of 13,298 words.

Respectfully Submitted,

April 25, 2013

Samuel H. Sloan
Administrator of Estate
of K. Michael Goodall
with Will Annexed
461 Peachstone Terrace
San Rafael CA 94903
(415) 419-5980
917-659-3397
samhsloan@gmail.com

IN THE COURT OF APPEAL OF THE STATE OF CALIFORNIA
No. A137739

SAMUEL H. SLOAN, Administrator of the Estate
of K. Michael Goodall with Will Annexed
Objector and Appellant,

v.

SAM WARE,
Movant and Respondent,

and

Bank of America, N. A. Plaintiff

Verification:

Sam Sloan declares:

I have read the Appellant's Brief I filed in this matter, and I declare under penalty of perjury under the laws of the State of California and the contents thereof are true and correct to the best of my knowledge and belief.

DATED: April 25, 2013

Sam Sloan

CERTIFICATE OF INTERESTED PARTIES AND CERTIFICATE OF SERVICE

Pursuant to California Rules of Court, Appellate Rules, Rule 8.208 the following is a list of parties who have appeared in this case or are interested in the outcome of this case. This includes all of the surviving Brothers and Sisters of Kenneth and Rachel Goodall and for those who have not survived their known children and grandchildren. I hereby state that on April 25, 2013 I served a copy of this Appellant's Brief by mail to all of the following:

Gary D. Rothstein
Manatt, Phelps & Phillips, LLP
One Embarcadero Center, 30th Floor
San Francisco CA 94111

Alicia A. Adornato
Attorney for Guide Dogs for the Blind
Reed Smith LLP
101 Second Street, Suite 1800
San Francisco CA 94105

Guide Dogs for the Blind
Mr. Thomas Horton
Planned Potential Beneficiary Giving Director
Guide Dogs for the Blind, Inc.
350 Los Ranchitos Road
San Rafael, CA 94903

Sam Ware
700 Larkspur Landing Circle, #199
Larkspur, CA 94939

John L. McDonnell, Jr.
Reed Smith LLP
1999 Harrison Street, 24th Floor
Oakland CA 94612

Don A. Lesser
1010 B Street Suite 350
San Rafael CA 94901

Jerry R. Hauser
Miller Hauser Law Group
4 Embarcadero Center, 39th Floor
San Francisco, CA 94111

James R. Hastings
1003 3rd Street
San Rafael, CA 94901

Robert J. Rothman
601 California St Suite 1600
San Francisco, CA 94108

Deborah Rodgers
Bradley Luxury Division
851 Irwin Street
San Rafael CA 94901

Roy Hoppe
461 Peachstone Terrace
San Rafael CA 94903

Frank Thornally
461 Peachstone Terrace
San Rafael CA 94903

Julia Bentley Lemons
Apt. 308
12800 Marion Lane W
Minnetonka, MN 55305-1368
Surviving Sibling of Rachel Goodall

Robert B. Bentley
Timberwood Senior Living Rm. #34
5020 WE 44th St.
Oklahoma City, OK 73135

Helen Beth Bentley Perry
7926 Praver Drive W
Jacksonville,FL 32217
Surviving Sibling of Rachel Goodall

Clenda Fern Bentley Zinar
4536 Chatman Street
The Colony, TX 75056

Beverly Gale Bentley Young
2316 Trenton
McKinney, TX 75070

Vickie Bentley Hankins
14580 NE 6th
Choctaw, OK 73020

Jeffrey Bentley
4701 N Douglas Boulevard
Spencer, OK 73084

Chad Everett Bentley
1609 Teepee Trail
Kingsland, TX 78639

Jeanette Goodall Phillips
152 S llth Street
Salina, Kansas 67401

Kristin Kane
University of California
Berkeley College of Engineering
College Relations
208 McLaughlin Hall #1722
Berkeley, CA 94720-1722

Bank of America
1000 4th St.
San Rafael, CA 94901

Made in the USA
Monee, IL
08 November 2026

67383086R00037